Ringing the Changes

poems by

Kathleen McCoy

Finishing Line Press
Georgetown, Kentucky

Ringing the Changes

Publisher: Leah Maines

Editor: Christen Kincaid

Cover Art: Kathleen McCoy

Author Photo: Kathleen McCoy

Cover Design: Elizabeth Maines McCleavy

Printed in the USA on acid-free paper.
Order online: www.finishinglinepress.com
            also available on amazon.com

Author inquiries and mail orders:
Finishing Line Press
P. O. Box 1626
Georgetown, Kentucky 40324
U. S. A.

Table of Contents

Ordinary Time

As the deer pants for streams of water,
so my soul pants for you, my God.
—Psalm 42:1

for Bob, Lizzie, and the seeker in each reader

Dreams & Meditations

All night the dark buds of dreams open richly.
—Mary Oliver, "Dreams," *Dream Work*

Grace

For me, every hour is grace.
—Elie Wiesel

That recurring dream
where you pour yourself
a paper cup of arsenic

thinking it is water but
pause to question
before drinking and

watch the cup
melt before
your eyes can blink.

In dreams' liminal land

there is always some high-wire mission to perform
and something to remind you, you

are small as light shines down and always, there is
light on umber evenings, ombre rooms, amber hands,

light coming from you-don't-know-where. From your dark
eyes, your own distant feet. From those who speak

without any words. From random jasper and
conniving pine. From the chimney swift swiftly

flapping past your unsuspecting face. From shadows
too angularly distorted to reflect your true face.

From the footstool your father made. From distant
ground congealed with the blood of refugees.

From the body of the saint who visits in your sleep. From
just beyond the periphery of what you wish you could see

behind the blinding-backlit door. From within.
From whirling atoms, dark crevices that somehow

coalesce as chair, table, wall. You touched the casket once,
fingers lingering, and felt, saw vibrations of wood-atoms

and startled, live-wire alert. You see your rooms are glowing,
molecules whirling paisleys of light before your eyes so all

that's left when these kaleidoscopic dreams resolve
is to enter their shadows and spin.

Dream State

Perhaps life is . . . a dream and a fear.
—Joseph Conrad

Wrapped in flannel sheets, you close your eyes.
Breath like bellows feeds the fire behind them.
As at the holidays, gifts and horrors alternate

in sleep—the rollercoaster will not
stop, you fly over the Alps in snow, swim
lithely in the Amazon, emerge naked

to the laughter of everyone at work. Black
satin gloves on disembodied hands seem pleased
to be invited to the garden. A handsome

terrorist drops a welcome mat of excrement at your feet.
Your car's on fire. It isn't your car. Celebrities and poets
shadow you, chattering with Thich Nhat Hanh.

You lose your wallet, find it, lose it again;
this time it's given back. Footprints appear on your walls
like runes. Spiders fall from webs all around you,

bees swarm, ants trek out of every crevice in the house.
You learn lines from a book you've never read, then can't
recall your lines or even what play you're in this time

as you're about to make your entrance. When you ask
to speak to God, angels resembling school counselors
point to a static-spewing monitor. You watch your hands

as they're meticulously deboned, sit in on lectures
in the classroom of the dead. Your shadow
sticks to the soles of your shoes. Pigs stampede.

Spectacles of color and sound dance across the cave wall.
A towering white-robed androgyne speaks like waterfalls
that vibrate from scalp's shuddering follicles.

In walks Jesus, crouching in his Levis, fingering dirt.
You're advised to cast no stones at shadows,
keep your wallet in your hands and know

what swine are for. You let your shadow kill the pigs.
You eat their pink flesh, let it feed the corpuscles,
muscles, gray matter, dark matter that feels

light-years away, that lives inside your skull.
A gypsy hands you a coiled cobra and you
lean toward it, surprised to feel no fear.

Little Buddha

The foot feels the foot when it feels the ground.
—Buddha

Brown ladybugs at sill and sink
jaunt, trudge, dream round

red dreams. I've utterly no idea
what leaves they need to nibble on,

how long they'll walk on porcelain
and wood. One, a drop of nutmeg,

shows off black-stocking legs, wobbliest
of can-can dancers. One leg's

missing. As it tumbles sinkward
I scoop a rescue. It seems

to contemplate its fate, accepting,
as I offer her or him a drop

of water, let little Buddha be.
Hours later, it hasn't moved. I flick it

down the porcelain vortex, wish it well
as it slinks into the sink's slick drain.

Learning to Pray

*People wish to learn to swim and at the same time
to keep one foot on the ground.*
        —Marcel Proust

I had friends whose parents
taught swimming by tossing them in
the creek or pond or pool's deep din.
Haunted inexplicably
by fear of deep water,

I cannot say I've always chosen
the deep end when I've thrashed in there,
but a moment before, limbs quaking mid-air—
oh, the joy of simply jumping
into strong and wide-flung arms.

The Parable of the Blanket

*And even as I cover myself with the tallit in this world, so may my soul
deserve to be clothed with a beauteous spiritual robe in the world to come
in the garden of Eden.*
—Morning prayer from the Siddur

It was as if they had said, *I shall wear my body by day
and yours by night.* She pressed her back gently into him
and he enfolded her; they warmed (their double heat
softening their shells) and as they drew close

they saw the threads that linked them wove
a blue blanket which covered their bodies,
stretching beyond their feet (growing softer,
richer-hued, extending inexorably): *Look*—

it's covering the cat, they said as the blanket crept
toward the chest (past plants, approaching the door,
passing beneath it and beyond) as easily
as smoke. The longer they wore it,

the farther it went (more social than they, more
inviting, more serene), yet somehow
chilling—the thought that even then it was
caressing sticky sores of strangers on the street,

warming dirty fingers, bandaging bloody limbs—
they made up their minds (if not their bed) to follow it
to places they'd scarcely thought of, where reporters
recorded the news their friends would watch

(while consuming fish and salads on silver trays).
They washed the blanket, packed it, wrapped themselves in it
day after day until (their bones could feel) their bodies
had absorbed from it some of what was real.

Read My Lines

We had seen God in His splendors, heard the text that Nature renders.
We had reached the naked soul of man.
　　　—Sir Ernest Shackleton

"The World Is a Text," the battered
Camry's bumper simply states.
When I think I hear the world it says,
If you want to know me, read my lines.

Read my lines says the birch, playing
with the wind, watching itself coil
in skin-strips to the earth. *Read my lines*, says
the spider, stretching iridescent strings

like a child's game. *Read my lines*
say the *Zohar, Bible, Quran, Sutras*,
taking my hands, turning my palms
skyward. *I wrote you many times,*

love letters written with the pen of my flesh.
My lines are in your hands.
My ink is in your blood.
The hairs on your head are mine.

Meditation on Flight 692

*I said, "Oh, that I had the wings of a dove! I would fly away
and be at rest."*
—Psalm 55:6

Outside my window the descending sun
reflects its gold on a luminous layer of blue
and the pinkish outer folds of cumulus clouds
whose quiet vibrates with a billowing grace
that asserts itself surprisingly,

and I think if I must I could die right now,
for sun is pouring light upon the silver wing
as the plane tips beneath it like a teapot.
Below us, Atlanta unfurls its jazzbeat streets,
ivy-covered trees, smoky, soulful songs,

broken Coca-Cola glass and weathered signs
that *Jesus is the Shepherd* and *We Shall Overcome.*
Nearly palpable within these clouds—
Stone Mountain, the cragged Canyon, Painted Desert,
whitewashed Pennsylvania farms, Appalachian shacks,

Kentucky's sodden caves, Times Square's light,
two oceans, at least, and every place where
dust is free and prayer is the state of being
linked, through no more effort than love's
desiring, to the source of the unending

pulsebeat of all movement and all breath.
Two hours into flight, the night arrives
and Memphis looms below in swirls and lines—
canary, kelly green, white, crimson, blue—
subsumed in a quasar of enveloping blackness;

above, a deep blue sheath, then a light blue marks
this great divide on which we ride between the earth
and moon, drumming our fingers to rhythms
of engine and evening and pulse until the neon
confetti below breaks into dance on a mat of black.

This Side of the Horizon

". . . Even if your exiled people are at the farthest horizon,
I will gather them . . . ."
—Nehemiah 1:9*

A fog-cloaked farm wraps a smoky mantle about its neck
and writhes, teasing, then clouds separate as we climb the sky
to ride thick strands of twisted cotton candy
before they contort again, teased into a clown's bouffant,

then spill in wave after wave of white arcs
flash frozen in time, illumined at the top
while plots of squares and tufted grooves appear
in patches below, cartographer's fingerprints—

but then the mist rises, subduing the waves.
How far above the sweat and stink of land
we are, how high above the birthing girls,
dying men, cold caws of crows—and now

it's layer on layer on layer—surely we're launching
into some stratosphere of spirit. The piquant
gases are not mushroom clouds; we are
not riding angels' wings, and yet

our wings shoot lithely through space
as the moon looks down from its
silver thread and we rush headlong
toward our common star.

Student Teachers

He heals the brokenhearted and binds up their wounds.
—Psalm 147:3

I don't know anyone over twenty who isn't
brokenhearted. It's true that now, somewhere

a child is being beaten. Or a student is
carving lines into her iliac artery

with her boyfriend's Gillette. Another, filled up
on cheap beer and skag, rams his truck into an oak

on 149. His kin will never know if he knew
what he was doing. There's a seventeen-year-old

two exits down who's left home and ended up
with fishnets, salty skin, daily dough, no way out.

I know a young man's rage can swell so much
his face will contort into a horror-flick mask, leaving us

to wonder if a gun were in his bag, how long
we'd have. I've heard confessions, read pleas, seen

tires slashed, windshields slammed. Twice young men
have said it was a priest that held them down. In every

class, someone's story bleeds out on the page—
IED punctures pockmark a mangled leg;

seventy-three-year-old burns become crinkled sleeves
on a Nagasaki lady; serial numbers stamp a wrinkled arm.

Then there are the quiet ones whose wounds show
only in their eyes, who give themselves away

to parent a parent or a child's child. No one's pain
can be appropriated. Nor forgotten. Nothing

I can write will lower their pressure or soften their eyes.
We so often parse the line between insanity and evil

that I wonder if it's not a line at all, more
a maze constructed to run us into each other

in our frantic search for exits. We can run
each other down or stop, face each other,

feel our way together out of dark dead-
ends to an exit no one saw before.

If God is watching, I only know how much
we must have forgotten—shared stories, genomes,

our fear of the dark, dreams we abandon
like unwanted children on someone else's steps.

In Silence

for my students

> *That person is like a tree planted by streams of water, which yields its*
> *fruit in season and whose leaf does not wither—whatever they do prospers.*
> *—Psalm 1:3*

To see in a leaf
the handprint of mortality,

in a conch shell
the cornucopia of desire,

in a wisp of willow
the cascade of chaos,

in the depths of a lake
the reflection of awareness,

in a pine cone
the tree of life;

to call what is
its natural, Adamic name, and

from what-is to derive
pangs of wonder, depths of drive.

Waiting in Wonder / Advent Dreams

I saw in the night visions . . . .

—Daniel 7:13

Noah and His Retinue

As it was in the days of Noah, so it will be at the coming of the Son of Man.
—Matthew 24:37

Waters rise in darkness. Family vies
with giants when the lights grow dim
for the promise of an arc-lit sky.

In the drench and stench of the sty
when all feel seasick, dank and grim,
waters rising in darkness, they vie

for air, for water without brine.
The animals stomp, bleat, caw to him
who promised them an arc-lit sky.

Male and female jostle on the sly,
chew their cud, then can't stifle screams
for waters rise in darkness where they lie

for months, pride passing them by.
Flood-flushed giants drown in their dreams—
Noah awaits the promise: arc-lit sky,

the laughingstocks and their livestock dry,
raising the olive branch, their hymn.
Waters recede like darkness. Why?
The promise. Love's blood. Arc-painted sky.

Dreaming of Showtime

*I have set my rainbow in the clouds, and it will be the sign
of the covenant between me and the earth.*
—*Genesis 9:13*

How many times a year do I pray for a sign
while passing open palms, hungry eyes, skywriters,
headlines about refugees, dry folks left to mutter,
shuffling ones who rarely look up as they pass,

shivering children, clumps of pierced
and lonely teens, feckless folk
who cast aspersions like brass doorstops
upon their mates' lowered heads?

Yet once again I prayed for peace
and for a sign about my role. That night
I dreamed I ran backstage in an ever-
expanding multiplex, calling for the director—

wasn't it showtime, after all? No one
had time to explain. Theatre A, replete
with ballerinas mid-arabesque; Theatre B,
the Army-Navy game *en medias res;*

Theatre C, Cordelia convicting Lear; Theatre D,
a live newscast, and on—some in overture, some
near intermission, others near the end—orchestrated
by a single director who knew all the parts,

all the plays, all the options, all the cues. No curtain
could be heavier than the one we would send falling
if we refused our parts. There was no audience but God.
When I woke I knew the meaning of *salam* and *shalom*—

both action and being in balance in the now,
fractured fault lines healed across the world.

Winter Dreams

He shall come down like rain upon the mown field,
like showers that water the earth.
　　　　　—Psalm 72:6

When night enfolds me in its woolen clasp
the air chills thickly, stars
recede beyond my gaze and I forget
the sound of a voice in the trees
the brush of a finger on my cheek
the glow of sun upon my neck

the press of feet on earth beside me
then I dream I'm soaring above
the timberline where angels dash
dreams coalesce the world is wrapped
in woven blankets heaven hits the hold button
to hear from us of our need for signs

On dark and winding paths dead wood
desires to be pruned back to greenness
gratitude rises like fog for wind that stokes
the fire, snow that falls in drought
poignance of casual notes found
after the writer has moved on

eyes that look beneath veneer, the feel
of hand on hand vision of a world
where our notes no longer clash, where
every person's tree of life
unfurls bursting with fruit
and judgment drifts away

Larval Dream

We say there are miracles of transformation
so long as we can pin them down to beauty parlor,

cosmetic counter, operating room.
Don't you sometimes wonder

whether miracles materialize in court
or in the elbow-laden loneliness of malls,

crowded classrooms, markets, or perhaps
in smudged mirrors of the self?

Just once in a dream I looked down upon
my own chrysalis in fetal position,

lying in the bed in white translucence, thin,
brittle like molted snakeskin or vacant conch,

and sprang up, shocked awake
by a flutter that lightens and lifts.

Meeting Gabriel

The angel answered, "The Holy Spirit will come on you, and the power of the Most High will overshadow you."
—Luke 1:35

I was reaching for the clay pot when I sensed
a stranger in my father's house I tried to scream
tried to pitch the pot and send it crashing on his head

I could not move I could not scream When he said
Don't be afraid I simply dropped my fear
He was the kind of man a wild horse could love

I thought he was don't laugh—an angel
There was a calmness in his eyes I seemed to float
to walk upon shadows standing on the other side

of God separated by my frailty until
it fell from me like old skin A mirror filled
with a light so intense I could see beyond myself

I heard a murmur rise from my throat
and when the room flooded hot the sudden thrumming
whir of nightjars shattered a careful silence

I heard the cries of fallen women
My belly filled with human hunger human grief
In a red rush I pleaded for my people with all

my being beyond words marveling with the palms
how the whole of language intervenes and yet
our silence grows

Mary's Awakening

I was a girl who scarcely knew my own blood.
Don't you recall your ungainly limbs, boundless,
gnawing energy? Anything is possible

though soldiers tramp the streets that outcasts line,
though proud men hog the courts and the hungry
hold their signs with quiet pleas—nothing is impossible—

the desert will burst into bloom. The poor
will be seated at the table overflowing with spiced meats,
figs and goblets of wine as the rich are turned away;

the servants faithful on their knees will discover
their full height. God lifts the chins of all
who hide in musty rooms where women pray,

where children worry and men lie low.
Darkness will disappear as if night had never been
and the presence of I Am will reach each war-torn,

pock-marked place on the map, for any town
will do, any soulful start is sufficient,
any small seed bears in its core the light

that created the world and saves it from itself.
I am boggled. I am small. I am blessed beyond belief.
My heart is glass to magnify the word, to shatter

at a word, my belly the dark center
that carries a glowing globe to the world.
The spirit that moved over waters of the deep

has moved in mine. And I am just the field's flat reed
the shepherd plucks to play for his sheep.
Heart's core opens at will, the globe glows. *Aloho!*

Sometimes you have to sing, to breathe, to utter God's *hadar*.
Love unfolds the petals of Sharon's rose. We have waited
since the desert burned our mothers' skin away.

Joseph's Dream

Wizened, world-weary, splinters
embedded in my fingertips, *shema*
inscribed on my heart, I'm a poor man

who corrects every warp of wood with gentle bracing,
who coaxes wayward boards into straight planks,
who asks so little—a sturdy home, a faithful wife.

I meet in this dream an angel, though mostly
I see the face, radiant as the *shekinah*, a face
you can depend on, that sees every shim

and yet proceeds to change his mind about—
only everything—that convinces me to place
right over honor, a simple, bloated girl

above myself. I could burn with insult,
but in place of pain, a pang. Stepping
out of the wood, I see each cedar

sizzle brightly from within. I marvel
how the stillness and the dream have stirred
hearth's embers. I have seen farmers

go hungry but I have also seen
the *malach* from whom I will not turn.
For the first time, my first duty is joy!

Love has burst into the husk of this house.
My blood courses; my thinking has never been clearer.
The flesh of my hands peels like petals.

Immanuel will not just be with us—his face
will shine, his hand inscribe *love* on the stiff
parchment where I feel it—here.

Dare Us

Now is your time of grief, but I will see you again and you will rejoice,
and no one will take away your joy.
             —*John 16:22*

The night is growing late. Do you hear
the vague rumbling, quiet cries
of those who long to exchange the world
                that ignores the scourged of Syria,
the bombed of Babylon for the world
of spirit begotten by a whisper,
a word become a note, a resonating tone
        that vibrates in the listener's chest?

It hums in the heart even now, kinnor
strings plucked by shepherds and kings
in wonder and worry, rage and praise.
                God of music, God of space,
whose dark energy eludes us, makes us
wait, compel us to imagine the closed strings
that permeate your errant world, bring
        kingdom home to us, among us and within.

Dare us to rejoice, to savor the sweet tang
of pomegranates ready to spill their round
red arils from their grotto of fruit!
                What can we do but wash ourselves,
offer our extra coats, submerge these fruits'
red globes, proffer their seeds? Cyclamens'
blazing petals surround their starry leaves.
        Ahava! God belts out, whoever's listening.

Dream of the First Face of Christmas

And she gave birth to her firstborn, a son.
—Luke 2:7

She takes his workman hand and steps away
from her angelic apparition into the cave's dark
stench and shuffle. Sunspots fill her soft

eyes. A child is coming, body and soul—
her hands will feed him, change him, her eyes
watch him become the one so long awaited.

She huffs like a broodmare crouching in the dark
as the inner shining sharpens its long red edge
inside her. At the end of her most trying night,

she gazes at two loves, exhaustion
their shared mantle. She swaddles one,
inscribing in memory the boy she knows

she doesn't know at all, whose touted launch
will shadow all her days. Bloody love has
split her at the seams, and when she turns

to touch his blood-streaked face, he looks cocooned,
marooned, aware that he has swallowed the moon,
tides rising in his eyes.

Dream of the Magus

After Jesus was born in Bethlehem in Judea, during the time of King Herod,
Magi from the east came to Jerusalem . . . .
  —*Matthew 2:1*

We step onto a winding path we've never seen before
        at the base of the dunes of our half-lived lives
                to follow heaven's estuary wherever it may lead,

leaving all behind but bread, presents, colleagues,
        the ash of our own fingerprints. As wind
                chills and night grows deeper in its blue,

we calibrate in the language of the stars their brilliance,
        their portents, wending our way westward
                on the unraveling broadloom coat of road

until its edges fix at last upon phosphorescent hues
        of the fresh-decoded, many-pointed star
                into whose silent flame we'd gladly fall,

beacon that pulses in the veins, that loops all ends
        into a Möbius strip of light that flows toward the men
                we are, mere points of light in the heaven of light

to which we shall return. Even now the boy's potent eyes
        remain when I shut my own, forbid us to return
                by the way we came, impel us to love all other eyes.

Dreaming of Jesus

> *. . . They are all mute dogs, they cannot bark; they lie around*
> *and dream, they love to sleep.*
> —Isaiah 56:10

He saunters in with his peristaltic
stare and greets me again in silence

as I sleep. Nothing brings
his visage wholly into focus,

nothing makes him flinch—
my confessions, tarred

speech, chained thoughts,
droll news, dreams of dread.

Every gift I offer turns to mud,
every word I try to speak

turns to ash upon my tongue
and still he smiles without recoiling.

I shake my head at how the mute,
heat-driven dogs of yearning and shame

wrangle behind me on the road where I face
headlights of the car he drives toward me.

Lent / Pasch / Passover

The wound is the place where the Light enters you.

—Rumi

Ashes

Therefore I despise myself and repent in dust and ashes.
—Job 42:6

Ashes kill weeds as well as they feed your plants,
stain shirts or clean your grime,
require soap before they render soap.

Crossed annually on the forehead
they become the phylactery of death,
finger-string reminder of its immanence,

bitter taste and shocking silkiness,
how it smudges everything it touches,
purifies the soil it settles upon,

fills the lungs with the thick volcanic silt
that shrouded Pompeii and Liberty Street,
washing humanity in uniform gray.

This year as we feed the palm-frond fire
the kindling of neglect—encouragement left
unuttered, greetings left unsent, bitterness better left

untasted—an incendiary flash: desire
that all we would cremate may serve
as the ashen bed from which we'll rise again.

Jeremiah's Covenant

I will put my law in their minds
and write it on their hearts.
I will be their God,
and they will be my people.
—Jeremiah 31:33

In the wadi of this wilderness
       after many years of pressure from the earth

this clay from which you formed my flesh grew
       petrified, unfeeling rock.

Agonies of spinning, sightless, pressed,
       in exile—now you make of me

a living fountain. Go ahead and write,
       in blood, your word upon my heart,

my hand will be within your own
       the pen. Soon you will draw nearer

than the space between my ribs.
       I hear you in the sun-dried wadi's wail for rain.

Now I know you as the one that sutures ruptured flesh
       in night's long ache for sunlight.

You grow us like seeds in the wadi of your body,
       you yank open the door our guilt had slammed.

At the feast you teach the measure from mouth to heart—
       the distance from wilderness to paradise.

Climbing Stairs under Daniel and the Angel

after Alek Rapoport's The Angel Opens the Eyes and Mouth of the Prophet,
relief/mixed media on plywood, 1991

Dimensions jag and roll, snatching
the moment time collapses. Red roils.
En route as I am to students, stacks, computers,

I think no lion wrests such stunned silence
as the angel's face of light, an arc
of blood blazing on its mouth.

Assumptions molt, ragged, blue.
White-haired Daniel, too decrepit to hike,
huddles on wrinkled knees—sackcloth radical

who'd sung in the furnace unsinged,
who'd stared down kings and lions—
praying for the exiles who would not

reclaim home. Beyond the frame,
I imagine others backing out,
unseeing, hiding from the quaking

glare, the power, the rift.
Why envy an encounter
whose secrets come gripping agony?

Perhaps to know that heaven will hear,
bend, touch. To hear the river rustling
a name or sign of the divine.

Nicodemus

The wind blows wherever it pleases. You hear its sound, but
you cannot tell where it comes from or where it is going.
So it is with everyone born of the Spirit.
　　　—John 3:8

I gazed into his dark eyes
that shone like a lantern in a stall.
What must I do, I blurted out,

when the old sacrifices get us nowhere,
the sellers of acceptable sacrifice clink with gold,
soldiers' boots nearly trample us and

though I glimpse the curtain of the inner sanctum
I am not allowed to enter? What prayers
suffice? What sacrifice will do?

To say his voice was steady is too simple;
to say I heard the thunder is too much,
but when I longed for a miracle, he said,

I shall enter the belly of a whale and emerge.
He said, *Be born of both water and spirit*—but how?
Can I return to the womb? *Think of* pneuma,

he said, *the wind. You see those olive branches*
and our hair flying without human touch?
So can you see when the Spirit blows.

You shall live in a country
without borders; you shall take off
the soiled robes of language; you shall bathe

in unpolluted water; you shall rise shining
if only you lie down upon the wind
and listen to the silent voice of God.

Sometimes I'm Jonah, sometimes the whale.
But always when I think of that night
a candle seems to flicker in my head;

I feel I'm lighting out on a firm wind,
then there is a plunging like a knife
somewhere in the center where it sears.

At the Well

The Samaritan woman said to him, "You are a Jew and I am
a Samaritan woman. How can you ask me for a drink?"
—John 4:9

At Jacob's well he came for a drink
and I felt my own parched throat
as the sun blared down;

he saw in my eyes
the old dirt and named it
without flinching,

then held up a glass for me
to see my shadow self
and said it was I

who should be asking
for water. Puzzled, I hoisted
the bucket up from the well

and he spoke of a green fountain
springing without end. I owned
the dark well of my past

but he broke that wall.
My secrets embodied—
he saw through my curves

and asked me, finally,
for nothing—change
would come like the tide

if I would drink new water. I said
I'd take his tonic as the sun blared down
but he knew I didn't understand at all.

He who had nowhere to lay his head
could overflow my jar with a word.
Years later, I can say without blushing

he pulled down the scarlet curtain of my shame,
forced to budding my stubborn cells
when I saw myself with his eyes.

The Day the Trees Laughed

> *He looked up and said, "I see people; they look like trees*
> *walking around."*
> *—Mark 8:24*

From my rag-seat on my bed of stone
I scrambled, always falling
in my dreams. As I clanged my cup

I heard footsteps withdraw
but he drew near
who makes a salve of spit

and a balm of mud; shapes
from words and a town of talk;
a standing, sighted, useful man

from clay damp with darkness.
I only know the coin-weight rose
when the lead curtain was lifted

from my eyes and I woke up
to a world I thought I knew
but could no longer call my own.

The black birds flapped away.
You might as well have clanged a gong
against your once-deaf ears—the light

was so bright I do believe
the trees were laughing
and clapping their hands!

Now it's good to see but strange
to chew the flesh of fruit
and behold the orchard budding,

to watch the sighted wander
and the hearing cock their heads,
dazzled, dazed by nature's designs,

odder still to witness
glory blazing without sense
so even *I* can see.

The Sixth Sign

> *Jesus wept . . . . Jesus called in a loud voice, "Lazarus, come out!"*
> *The dead man came out, his hands and feet wrapped with strips of*
> *linen, and a cloth around his face.*
> *—John 11:35, 43*

Mary

Something has yanked the rug.
My tongue is dry. Is dirt.
Resin the days, sewn up

the nights of pleas
as wine turns into vinegar
and bread molds.

The land grows still and stale.
With a word, without a sign
we wait. Our sobs turn into wails.

Martha

These hands grown stiff with pleas
used to knead. The vats have all
run dry. The bony figs all reek.

My ever-moving feet and hands
grow cold in summer's heat.
The space between us spreads like sands.

In all his years of heady talk
he never warned us
how long the heart can lock.

Lazarus

Feet dream-slipping, I sighed,
my breath grown heavy in the night.
Slowly my chest calcified

and, pulled past slipping, I fell darkly.
In my sleep I see who cannot see.
Now, from drowsiness, a key

cry, the ray that halts an endless dark
awakens like a bell. These bindings
cannot hold. It's burst or walk.

Bitters and Palms

They took palm branches and went out to meet him, shouting,
"Hosanna!"
—John 12:13

From Olivet on west to the feast
a scene as unexpected as a dream—
folks from every tribe, a throng

hard pressed, most days, to get along
join the parade, peeling off
their coats to close the dust

like curtains; little ones who must
be exhausted from their hike
hoist green maror, lower palms,

begin a chorus of familiar psalms,
Blessed is he who comes in the name of the Lord,
Hosanna! and, with an ass for his steed rides

the Man-with-No-Bed, the one Death heeds
whose eyes are wings of longing,
whose furrowed-brow smile

seems drawn from sorrow's well
to gift the unrelenting wildness of the world,
who sees the little failures of our days—

how freely all we who praise
jump on to ride the heavy blade
that chops the life from the lamb.

After Hanging Rembrandt's *Christ*

I gaze upon your gaze, transfixed,
your hands, tawny, shadowed, sure,
your eyes again, mesmerized, and now

I've *got* them so well I wouldn't really
have to look again, and yet I will, each
time I pass by, though sometimes

I fail, glance only at your hand,
the left, unhidden one, or the earthen
tones that surround you,

the glowing gold about a mat of brown,
the subtle strokes of red,
or the hair, longish, natural,

as simple as your presence is monolithic,
rumbling like the organ's bass
despite what I don't see—

instead of halo or angelic throngs
a genuine gaze, the rippling
lake of your look,

lips that do not lie—these deliver
shivers of gentian, inspire gestures
of acknowledgment—I hung you there,

I want you there—I take it back—I can
do nothing, all I do is here and
now, is dust upon the table,

tension in the spine, a terrible taste
on the tongue, and yet I look again,
again, again—I see

your bloody wrists, your damp hair,
the truth—I hung you there, but
still you look me in the eyes.

Vespers

Some say that we shall never know, and that to the gods we are like the flies that the boys kill on a summer's day, and some say, to the contrary, that the very sparrows do not lose a feather that has not been brushed away by the finger of God.
—Thornton Wilder, The Bridge of San Luis Rey

1

Now the tiny flock is sleeping in the nest
after hours of complaining. At last
their mom flew in, mouth full of grubs.

They kept their young throats open, she fed them
from the pantry of her mouth and now they sing
though their singing, their lives will not last long.

I, too, am small, hungry, temporary,
aching, weary of complaining.
Fill me up this evening. Sing

to me, rock the nest gently
with your feet, let me rest
in peace upon your down.

2

All my longing wells up
with the thirst of one whose canteen
sprang a leak the instant she hit the desert.

I carry heavy, splintered wood;
my arms ache. Yet this is all I have
to lay now at your feet.

3

Sweet Jesus, I love this part, where you
stack this useless heap, where the work
of your hands lights a spark and the wood

crackles glory, flames shooting up, then, slowly
smiling, you extend your hands, you pull me in
as the song sparrows croon.

Mary at Golgotha

Near the cross of Jesus stood his mother . . . .
—*John 19:25*

1

That the end would be like the beginning, windy,
fatherless, seems a thing you've always sensed.
A cross has dropped hard to the ground

wearing your body, leaving its beast-mark
branded on your back, with a prayer
for the patience it takes to find

mercy in a mob that cries for blood
in voices guttural as geese.
A steady procession of voices

cascades through the air with the trouble
of a captive sleep. They've pinned you
like an insect, nails cleave

the slim bones of your wrists. You have
to think to keep yourself from pain: I think
of Sychar, of the woman there who spoke of you,

who cradled a pail in her arms, her shock
at your Jewish skin, how her hair
stole out from its muslin, how you

could see her lovers
rising in the mist to touch her,
one after another.

2

A familiar face floats in the crowd—
the boy who gave his lunch away.
He tugged you down to his whisper, *I feel*

the orange sun rising in my chest.
You turn at a familiar voice but
your muscles arc in spasm.

Eli, Eli, the twisted face of the thief
seems a face you've always loved,
that knows the loneliness of birth.

They laugh. They think you can't see God
in their faces, that you mutter to yourself, a fool,
snake, illusionist, wizard and leader of witches,

soaking up praises of wretches like the sponge
of sour wine that levitates before you.
My God, preserve us from hatred.

3

This is how you must die?
Forever falling in the sound
that is always, voices of the dead,

falsity of fear, the waiting stone,
my "lovely" grating smile I send
with all the strength I can afford?

Listen. They cannot kill this cord.
But oh, you do look odd to me,
a stranger, a skeleton for a son.

4

The fists pound in my eyes, you rock me
with the seizure of your love,
wash me as I washed you. Long ago you ran

crying to me that another child
had called you *bastard*—I touched your head
and pulled you to me until I felt as real as anyone

but as soon as bread-scent wafted, you pulled away.
And once, as I dished out lentils, you looked into me,
your eyes smooth with the distance of water.

Carp never tasted finer.
When we were finished, you stood
before us like a priest, furrowed your brow,

then walked out. You stayed outside for hours.
I didn't cover my head. When you came back,
gray as a bird, no one said a word.

5

Would to God these nails
wouldn't split your gentle head,
you couldn't see me driven to hell

on the back of your wooden beast.
If this is a dream, let us both waken soon.
Son, I can't let go of you,

I cannot bear it. Our cups are full
but we can only drink our own.
I want to pull you down. Forgive me.

May John's be your arm around me,
though I am unclean too. My blood
riles in disgust. There is no help,

my body sinks like many yet to come
who deserve no thrashing, no lynching;
their cries sharpen their blades on us.

6

This is the hardest birth,
caught in the womb of the world,
amid the clamor of men and beasts

to thrash like a drowning woman
as her eldest thrashes under nails.
This scene I see keeps altering—

slanting into slats that slide out of focus—
now a thin green curtain sparkles:
men are walking trees; horses, living rocks.

I feel like falling, I say a prayer.
Impaled on voices, you heave for air.
You must hang on, I must listen as you hang.

If madness is the brain swimming into itself,
then I am nearly mad. I follow
the motion forward and the pulling in again.

My God, how dare you leave us now?
I hear the crest and fall of dead seas,
children whimpering for bread,

keening moans of women at the grave—
strange possession—sounds of the drowned, voices
like the thunder of the waves, the grinding

chains of madmen, voices caught in the ear
on Peter's sword, the clack of a cup scraping bars,
cries calling from too many skins of history

with loud, hoarse sounds and the sound of hands.
The voices of their sins, our sins.
I have nothing. You have given me away.

I wear your every gesture, breath and tongue.
You breathe to the roughness of the world's hands;
your senses must be keener than a blind man's.

7

When they're hungry and their babies wail,
they will speak to you of hunger. When their sons turn
on each other, they will speak to me of pain.

When they stop to slake their thirst, when they
let the storm pass through them, when
they think they can't contain their dram

of joy—they will speak to us.
Our voices rise in you. You cannot die.
You have become us. All.

First Account: Mary of Magdala

Mary Magdalene went to the disciples with the news: "I have seen the Lord!"
—John 20:18

What is it to lose the rags that clothe your soul?
Telling the tale could hang me—still, he drove out
my despair so I would not flee from his

though darkness hurtled like boulders,
sky poured, earth quaked, roaring
as the temple curtain rent. Toward the black abyss

he dropped his head. We saw him through our rain.
I stood on anvils of clay, my arms pungent
with myrrh for his last anointing. The colossal

disk of stone was shoved away. *That*
was my final straw. Anyone could see us
wracked with sobs. In morning glare, standing

on a bloody carpet of anemones before stalks
of bluebeard, the gardener asked me why I cried,
but his face was snow in sleeting showers

as the sun embraced his form;
his eyes, familiar, widened—his pupils
were oceans, his irises worlds—

my vision cleared; scales molted away. I fell
to kiss his feet. The moment enfolded me—
red corn poppies, mouths of purple iris,

almond blossoms' open palms,
trembling trumpets of lilies!
As he returned the innocence of pain

I heard meaning's strange accent:
he had left his linen shroud, bearing
wounds I longed to kiss.

In strong wind, under an edgeless sky,
he grabbed the raveled end of my own bindings,
twirled me once more from him to life.

Ordinary Time

We live in the world when we love it.

—Rabindranath Tagore

Glen Lake in November

Sky-grazing
birches meld
motion and stillness

in lake's mirror
filled with clouds
and lilies. Birch

branches, bare,
siphon strength
from roots that drink

from underneath
the withered crust
of earth a deeper

water. Ions
of fresh water
quicken in wind.

Inside my coat
I feel only
silent water

rhythmic as rain.
The geese sailed
early this year

for somewhere south
of enough, to even
more. A wedge

of light creaks open
between my eyes.
We all marvel

at bushes' thrushes who,
despite their observations,
persist in singing.

Amish Quilt

Squinting eyes could mistake it
for a stained glass window, rectangular
pieces like shards of violet because
we die a lot in ticks and tocks.

Red because we've said so much
but never quite enough. Orange
for our range of flagrant bloom.
Blue for what wind does to water.

Purple for the pastiche of hue
and cries we stifle as we stitch
our shards of selves together,
miter corners, place the squares

we're given in the middle. The shock
is how these pieces slanted on the bias
of our lives scatter prismatic brightness
on the blackness at their backs.

Community: June 26, 2015

after Community *by Sister Corita Kent, 1982*

*"We are either going to become a community or we are going
to die."*
     —Barbara Ward

From inside a cavern's black mouth
sky, sun, distant mountains stand
distinct in their right colors, yet

merge so mountains' blue, sun's
maize, sky's coral form segments
of purple, brown, deep green, converge

to resemble you and you and you
and me when, at close of another day
of bold strokes and vague threats, posters,

op-eds, black-and-whiting the right of all
to love, to be distinct and yet together, at last,
despite the boisterous blare—nature's brightness

catches us and we see the spectrum of light
where our auras touch.

Cleaning Heart

Vacuum me inside-out,
triplet God of light
and smoky skies, of grain,

gray bracken, dreidel,
dread, prattle, prayer—
fill this empty casing

with molten love, let it bubble,
mold it after your own,
fine as hand-blown glass,

resonant as a koan,
clean as any queen,
fine as any binary model

can describe, alive
as ancient elders.
Leave my bones

dry and chiming
in the shadows
of the valley

of the life
I used
to know.

Dream of the Dark Night of the Senses

> *I saw a long gold spear in [the angel's] hand and there seemed to be a flame*
> *at the tip. This he seemed to plunge into my heart repeatedly, until it reached*
> *into my very entrails. When he drew it out, I thought he would draw them out*
> *with it, and it left me completely afire with a great love for God.*
> —*St. Teresa de Avila*, Life, Chapter XXIX

Saint Teresa de Avila dream-runs in and out
of the strange-familiar house past twilight
driven by desperation in darkness,

trying to recall some distant prayer
one can only pray when searching
in the night for the one she loves.

Walls breathe. Floors creak.
She dashes into a great gallery
full of virgins—terrible fakes,

she thinks, their bodies molded
in pious gestures. She gapes,
confused. But then the one with feet

of flesh and red roses draws her gasp.
Buckling at the knees on the threshold
of that room, she sees a dark cloud

of hooded angels with burning taper hearts
hovering. Her prayers at last return
quaking, fervent as a drowning child.

The tallest angel spears her from above
with a high-voltage bolt that lingers.
Red adoration sizzles in her breast.

The Respiratory Therapist with Cystic Fibrosis

No victim on the road to Jericho,
no fainting damsel, no petal-shedding rose,
no raucous star of hospital bed, no begrudging

laborer, she's learned to breathe through chest's
deep waters with music, with sun to free others' breath-
work when their lungs too grow sticky as honeycomb.

She tries not to measure her days but as she X's
each date off the month, her pace and pulse
quicken, sight lengthens, back straightens,

plans brighten. To bed by afternoon then
on her feet all night, she takes fresh air
with her everywhere, not to hoard but

to share, pushing practice in squeezing
the bellows, teaching the lungs
to rise, fill, fall, empty as others' do

without thought. With every breath she beams,
strengthened by the act of reaching the rattled
until her own lungs sputter-sputter red

and she is guided back to bed. Even then
she decorates the IV pole with a blow-up doll
that has more air than she does, laughing

as she coughs while you and I take for granted
the speech that comes with breath, our own hands'
grasp, various regular solaces—that fall will yield

to winter, winter to spring's clean-blowing
past the cold. Only when storms interrupt us
does our fancy flee so all we are holds on,

engages cogs of breath as daylight wanes, thunder
rattles winds upon the lake. The droll machines
churn on as sun cranks itself above faded horizon

that warms with rose-gold light, shadows
stretch, waters recede, mountains bow and raise
the rib cage in the breath of every prayer

we've ever prayed—that after this night of heavy air,
her muggy lungs and all the world's
will breathe, clean and whole and lighter, soon.

Elegy for a St. Louis Lineman

You should be blowing your whistle at the twenty-yard line
in your striped shirt or scaling a pole to fix the line or
popping a brew with a line of Navy vets or yelling

past the Cardinals' line home or showing the kids exactly
where the line *is* because you question lines, you kick them,
you dance them before you toe them

and lines begin to form behind you, for all who know you
long to follow you dancing the rock-'n-roll blues that pulse
in your veins, that pull your face into the ear-wrapping arch

gleaming as gallium—
you the lone lineman
no lines can contain.

Fire in Her Bones

Pastor Linda heard a bell that rang her to the bone
in the River Jordan, that heated open palms
until her eyes, her arms, her body shone.

She gave the Spirit grief, dreading to leave home,
but glimpsed the black-eyed Susans, let them calm
the ringing of the bell inside her bones,

confessed to family and friends how blown
she was from all that she had known. Each Psalm
soothed her tired chest and arms which shone.

Each child and saddened soul who's known
her saw her hug away the sense of overwhelm
at how the Spirit burns inside our bones

despite our salty tongues and chests of stone.
What she gave she didn't learn in school. Qualms
dissolved as her eyes, her arms, her body shone

through storms, despite the scarcely audible moan.
In my dreams she's full-term with Spirit in a moonlit cave.
She let the Spirit tend the fire in her bones
until her eyes, her arms, her being shone.

Ringing the Changes

What would be the value of a bell which was never rung? It rings out clearly,
it bears witness, it cannot speak without seeming like a call, a summons.
A great bell is not to be silenced.
              —Iris Murdoch, The Bell

We watch the hand bell player,   her ears poised, gloved hands
steady, internal metronome   underscoring conductor's

inscription of time's signatures   in air. We sit enthralled
at all that jars the bones.   After the fog has lifted

over this convincing hologram,   bells peal what is real—
bells we cannot ignore   sweep off diurnal business,

direct us to the source   of cauldron and clanger.
Suzu, bonshō, kane bells   call to prayer. Sufi bells signal

time to dance in dervish flurry.   Jerusalem bells tell ancient Hebrews
when the priest has entered   the Holy of Holies, robes jingling.

For slaves summoned   by masters back to the fields,
terror twitches through time.   From heft of ancient days

bells clang, engraved with holy   hush, secret Tetragrammaton.
Some bells summon spirits   of the dead. Sanctus bells

chime for host and chalice;   Celts toss bells into wells.
Papageno's glockenspiel   tinkles with delight at his prospect

of finding, at last, a wife.   In the '40s the carillon my mother hears
plays "Faith of Our Fathers,"   her father's favorite, without ringing,

sends her flying home   without clocking out
so she can feel her father's   silent grip, see his hazel eyes

one last time. Rosh Hashanah   bells sever pretense from person.
Yes, we doubt, we pine, we   misalign, we cower, we cede

our power, ring alarms, descry
why the bells are ringing,

all harms, raise our arms asking
though we know. Their toll

brands the bones of mortals,
hatching, matching, dispatching,

cannot be possessed, proclaims
or with muffled sounds

of a small bell laced to
horrifies us to learn

the finger of a buried body,
we buried her alive.

~ ~ ~

When a great bell grows
the music bleeds

a crack, that's where
its beauty as the light pours

through, pours over us
We spin in tintinnabulation

until our own pores soak it in.
as centuries clang.

Bells of all creeds, all
chime the euphonic

times, beyond all time,
tonic we crave, sing

the truth within us
teach us to touch

until we know the tune,
without clinging.

praying in the dark

for us with furrowed brows
who run out of time or just in time
whose feet

who loathe anyone
whose losses howl
who time the kill

who charge into flames for strangers
who find a beam and focus it
whose prayer is bright

let the muscles of our brows unknit
let them cleanse the crying ground
let crouching corners fill with light

let the flames sputter and utterly die
that the terrible rendings may cease
to us a stranger

us slowed by stiffness or denial
who are ground to powder
have gone groundless

unlike ourselves
who time how long it takes to heal
who crave revenge on strangers

who've scraped the dark's knife-edge
who pray in gray and white
or blocked

let the ashes mix with water
let groundlessness fade to memory
let jagged wounds close up

let love quench our thirst for blood
that no one ever again would be
that each breath might be a prayer

Meeting Christ

As I sat beneath stained glass before the bread and wine,
my morning scream at my young child resounded,
dumped me darkly, gutted, sinking—

he rose in me from thumb size up to my face
bat-whoosh *welcome-but-don't-look-at-me-like-this—*
but he was here I tell you

real as I am to you straight-on unplumbed
gouging gazing wordless man of longing
who does not turn away

knowing-eyed—in those deep eyes
globes whirled, whole galaxies—
I grew small cool as he grew tall grew warm

grew bright in me—his large left hand loomed
then lay on my collarbone—
I feel its weight—right here—

You Can Fall

*The people who weep before my pictures are having the same
religious experience I had when painting them.*
—Mark Rothko

You can fall into a Rembrandt, plow
into Picasso or sail into Kandinsky, but Rothko
requires a pause. As for you—I'm puzzled—

you look cloudy as Rothko,
mind-warping as Dali, embracing
as Merton, dogged as Teresa,

strong-spined as Mary, scorching as sun.
I have rolled right into Rothko but into you—
Orion of the drawn bow, shrinking space,

touching the untouchable,
laughing as the wine is poured—
into you, because my eyes were closed,

oh Christ, I've crashed—
but now, as my eyes open,
you help me to my feet.

Notes

The Parable of the Blanket

The *tallit* is a prayer shawl worn by observant Jews. The epigraph is the morning prayer from the *Siddur*, a book of traditional Jewish prayers.

Noah and His Retinue

This villanelle comes in because the Noah story sometimes comes up in the lectionary during Advent. Its story of promise and salvation from destruction presages that of the Christ.

Dreaming of Showtime

Salam is Arabic for *peace*; *shalom* is *peace* in Hebrew.

Mary's Awakening

"This [in the Magnificat] is not the gentle, tender, dreamy Mary whom we sometimes see in paintings; this is the passionate, surrendered, proud, enthusiastic Mary who speaks out here."—Dietrich Bonhoeffer. The Magnificat (Luke 1:46-55) echoes the Song of Hannah in the Old Testament (I Samuel 2:1-10), a victory song of the oppressed sung by a quadruply oppressed and disenfranchised human being: a woman, a pregnant woman (in Hannah's case, a formerly barren woman; in Mary's, an unwed girl), a poor person, and a Jew.
Aloho—Aramaic, *God's significance.*
Hadar—Aramaic, used as *magnificence, honor, majesty.*

Joseph's Dream

"But after he had considered this, an angel of the Lord appeared to him in a dream and said, 'Joseph son of David, do not be afraid to take Mary home as your wife, because what is conceived in her is from the Holy Spirit.'" — Matthew 1:20

Shema—Hebrew for "hear," the opening word of the foundational text of Judaism (Deuteronomy 6:4-9): "Hear, O Israel: The Lord is our God, the Lord alone. You shall love the Lord your God with all your heart, and with all your soul, and with all your might." *Shekinah* (also *Shekhinah*)—according to the Jewish Virtual Library, "The *Shekhinah* is a Talmudic concept representing God's dwelling and immanence in the created world. It was equated with the '*Keneset Yisrael*,' the personified spirit of the People of Israel." *Malach*—Hebrew for messenger; angel.

Dare Us

Kinnor—a stringed, harplike instrument played by King David. *Ahava*—Hebrew for *love*, from roots meaning *I give* and also *love*.

The Sixth Sign

The gospel of John is structured around the concept of signs that Jesus was the Jewish Messiah; the resurrection of Lazarus from the dead was the sixth sign.

Bitters and Palms

Maror is raw horseradish used in the Passover seder meal to symbolize the bitterness of slavery in Egypt.

Glen Lake in November

This poem is dedicated to the late Rev. Linda Hoeschle, who led a spiritual retreat at Glen Lake.

Community: June 26, 2015

This poem is dedicated to the Rev. Dr. Sheldon Hurst, who introduced me to the art of Sister Corita Kent. On June 26, 2015 the Supreme Court of the United States legalized marriage for all American couples.

Cleaning Heart

This poem was written for the Rev. Linda Hoeschle.

The Respiratory Therapist with Cystic Fibrosis

This poem is dedicated to Sharon Dingman, the force of nature who organizes the Music for Life benefit for CF research in Hudson Falls, New York.

Elegy for a St. Louis Lineman

This poem elegizes Gordon Aronoff, Jr.

Fire in Her Bones

This poem elegizes the Rev. Linda Hoeschle.

Ringing the Changes

Mawlana Jalal-al-Din Rumi's line "The wound is the place where the light enters you" informs the last part of this poem.

You Can Fall

In 1964 Mark Rothko was commissioned to create site-specific paintings for the chapel in Houston that bears his name and features fourteen large-scale tonal paintings for observers to focus on as they pray or meditate. Today this ecumenical chapel houses colloquia on human rights, drawing leaders from around the world.

Acknowledgments

Many of the poems in this volume have been previously published: *Tupelo Press 30/30 Project*: "Dream State," "Student Teachers," "Learning to Pray." *Mom Egg Review*: "Amish Quilt." Published in earlier forms in broadsides by First Baptist Church of Glens Falls, New York; Village Baptist Church in Fort Edward, New York, and/or Kingsbury Baptist Church in Kingsbury, New York: "Noah and His Retinue" (originally "Noah, His Crew, and His Retinue"), "Dreaming of Showtime" (originally "Showtime for Peace"), "Larval Dream" (originally "What Do You Dream?"), "Winter Dreams," "Meeting Gabriel," "Joseph's Dream," "Dare Us" (originally "Daring to Rejoice"), "Dream of the First Face of Christmas" (originally "Mother Dreams"), "Dream of the Magus" (originally "Dream of a Modern-Day Magus"), "Jeremiah's Covenant," "Ashes," "At the Well," "Nicodemus," "The Sixth Sign," "The Day the Trees Laughed," "Bitters and Palms," "First Account," "After Hanging Rembrandt's *Christ*," "Glen Lake in November." "Meeting Christ" was anthologized in a Lenten booklet edited by the Rev. David Wood. *Expressions* published "This Side of the Horizon." *Ekphrasis: Art into Words* (Visual Arts Gallery, Adirondack Community College, 2009), an anthology edited by the author, published "Climbing Stairs under Daniel and the Angel." Originally printed in the poet's creative dissertation, *Losing the Rhythm for Holding the Notes* (Univ. of Missouri): "Meditation on Flight 692." Reprinted with permission from the poet's chapbook *Night-blooming Cereus and Other Poems* (Adirondack FemSoul Press, 2007): "Dare Us" (as "Daring To Rejoice"). The poem "praying in the dark" (originally published as "prayer for dark september") first appeared on the poet's blogs *The Real McCoy: A Take on Poetry* and *Poetry for Peace and Justice*.

Grateful acknowledgment goes to Leah Maines for accepting this manuscript; Christen Kincaid, my editor; Kevin Maines and Elizabeth Maines McCleavy of Finishing Line Press. Special thanks to Marilyn McCabe and Mary Sanders Shartle along with the rest of the WMD Poetry Group (Women of Mass Dissemination) for their wise counsel and literary conviviality: Nancy White, Dr. Elaine Handley, and Dr. Lale Davidson. Thanks to the Rev. Kathleen Davie, the Rev. Dr. Sheldon Hurst, the Rev. Caspar Green, the Rev. Dr. Don Shuler, the late Rev. Linda Hoeschle, the Rev. David Wood, and the Rev. Stephanie Schneider, who solicited, encouraged, and/or shared this work; to the Rev. Dr. Wayne R. Bruner, who included one of my poems in his thesis; Sharon Dingman, who dances on air; the late Jerry Dean, who urged me to publish this book; the churches named above; the monks, poets, and songwriters of Weston

Priory; my friends of the Jewish, Buddhist, Quaker, Methodist, Catholic, Presbyterian, Anglican, Episcopalian, Islamic, Unitarian Universalist, and other faiths or states of seeking; also the SUNY Adirondack Writers Project; the University of Rio Grande in Rio Grande, Ohio, and Caffe Lena in Saratoga Springs, New York. Thanks beyond measure to the late Paul Pines for sharing his Jungian wisdom and big-hearted support. Eternal thanks to my husband, Bob Medve; our daughter, Lizzie; my twin, Christine McCoy Bruner, and Bill and Alva McCoy for their love and support of my work.

Kathleen McCoy grounded the book you are holding in her work as a community college professor at SUNY Adirondack and her spiritual practice as a deacon. Her work has been published by *Sojourners, AROHO, Seasons of the Spirit, the National Council of Teachers of English, The American Baptist, Mom Egg Review, The 30/30 Project*, and other publications. Her first full-length collection, *Green and Burning*, was named finalist in the Book Excellence Awards (Canada); other work was commended by the Gregory O'Donoghue International Poetry Competition and the Fish International Poetry Awards (both in Ireland) and the Dana Awards.

Michael White has called *Green and Burning* "resonant and resilient . . . for any seeker in the realm of the spirit," and the late Paul Pines stated, "Whether McCoy's poems dance on the page or move without ornamentation, they always take us into the heart of the matter." Nancy White has written: "McCoy's controlled lines, alternately stately and frisky, make this commitment to the reader: to speak what matters. The female body, the mind and mortality of man, the unnamable-but-named God: these are her touchstones, but she never presumes to know all the answers. There's room for mystery here, and as in the work of feminists before her, the fierce is infused with the fertile and the smart."

McCoy lives in upstate New York with her husband, daughter, and the cats who own them. You can follow her blog, *The Real McCoy: A Take on Poetry* (http://kathleenmccoypoet.com), and she can be found on Twitter and Instagram @ kathmccoypoet.